I Wish I Had Said That...

I Wish I Had Said That...

Monica D. Davis

To Bridget,
All my best,
Monica D. Davis
Aug 29, 2021

For Jerry,
a Master Wordsmith,
who brings love and
wisdom to my life.

I Wish I Had Said That…

Here is a collection of perfect comebacks, well-articulated thoughts and sayings.
Use as you wish. Now you will no longer say "I wish I had said that," because now you will…

The title of this book comes from an exchange between James McNeill Whistler and Oscar Wilde. Whistler made a clever comment. At which Oscar Wilde said, "I wish I had said that." Whistler replied, "You will, Oscar. You will."

Staircase Wit

Words of the Staircase (French)

A term used for the predicament
of thinking of the perfect
comeback,
only too late.

Words one should have used,
realized only after leaving a
gathering,
on the staircase while exiting the
event.

Nothing so needs reforming
as other people's habits.

Dressed in a little brief authority.

A tortured relationship with the
truth.

Sunshine is the best disinfectant.

One always finds,
What one is looking for.

You are entitled to your own
opinion.
You are not entitled to your own
facts.

He is a modest person
with much to be modest about.

The tree falls... the monkeys
scatter.

I am sometimes bored by people
But never by life.

You are entitled to your
argument.
You are not entitled to win.

You are always responsible for
how you act,
no matter how you feel.

Incredible what you can
accomplish
when you do not care who gets
the credit.

Yesterday is not ours to recover,
but tomorrow is ours to win or
lose.

Not known to use words
which might send readers to the
dictionary.

Some cause happiness wherever
they go;
Others, whenever they go.

I have had a perfectly wonderful
evening…
But this was not it.

The reason I talk to myself
is because I am the only one
whose answers I accept.

Do you know
the last time I dined in this
restaurant?
Tonight.

Delusions of Adequacy.

Thank you for sending me your
manuscript.
I will waste no time in reading it.

Sometimes you win,
And sometimes you learn.

Miserable without you;
Almost like being with you.

Attention span of a lightning bolt.

They open their mouths,
to subtract from the sum
of human knowledge.

There is zero correlation
between being the best talker
and having the best ideas.

Extreme in his moderation.

Aging beautifully…
Nothing old but the jokes.

If I had two faces,
Why would I wear this one?

A strategy is nothing but good
intentions
unless effectively implemented.

I can explain this to you;
I cannot comprehend it for you.

Life is what happens
while you are making other plans.

He loves nature
in spite of what it did to him.

No idea is so outlandish
that it should not be considered.

Life is what you do
while you are waiting to die.

Thought:
Unfamiliar territory.

The reverse side
also has a reverse side.

A person of simple tastes.
Easily satisfied with the best.

Experts are people who know
more and more about less and
less.
Until they know everything
about absolutely nothing.

You go through life wondering
what it is all about.
At the end of the day
it is all about family.

Happiness
is not something you get in life.
Happiness
is something you bring to life.

A person who aims at nothing…
Is sure to hit it.

The human mind
is like a parachute.
It is of no use
unless it is open.

Size matters.
Who wants a small glass of wine?

The past is prologue.

The past is not past.

A library is a hospital for the mind.

I want it all,
and I would like it delivered.

Some things are better left unsaid.
Which I generally realize
right after I have said them.

Put some whiskey in coffee.
It is Ireland somewhere.

He has all the virtues I dislike
and none of the vices I admire.

Never ask a woman
who is eating ice-cream
straight from the carton
how she is doing.

I might wake up early and go
running.
I also might wake up and win the
lottery.
The odds are about the same.

Stop watering the weeds.

He is simply a shiver
looking for a spine to run up.

She is past her due date.

Often wrong.
Never in doubt.

It is not enough to wound the
enemy.
You must kill him.

God,
in creating man,
somewhat over-estimated His
ability.

Fashion
is what one wears oneself.
Unfashionable
is what other people wear.

A cynic is a man who
knows the price of everything
and the value of nothing.

Nothing ages like happiness.

Why do you sit there
looking like an envelope
without an address on it?

He has no enemies,
but he is intensely disliked by his
friends.

He uses statistics
as a drunken man uses a lamp
post…
more for support than for
illumination.

The only way to get rid of
temptation
is to yield to it.

He is not only dull himself;
he is the cause of dullness in
others.

The man who sees both sides of
the question
is a man
who sees absolutely nothing at all.

The clever people never talk.
The stupid people never listen.

Never put off until tomorrow
what you can do the day after.

I like to do all the talking myself.
It saves time and prevents
arguments.

Anybody can make history.
Only a great person can write
history.

Pity that in life
we get our lessons
only when they are of no use to
us.

One should always play fairly
when one has the winning cards.

If it wasn't for a double
standard…
They would have NO standard at
all.

Some disputes are so bitter.
Is it because
the stakes are so small?

After a good dinner
one can forgive anybody.
Even one's own relations.

Overthinking:
The art of creating problems that
don't exist.

Important to bring LIGHT
rather than HEAT
to the issues of importance.

Never Complain.
Never Explain.

Limousine Liberal.
Neiman Marxist
Salon Communist.

Any port in a storm.

Adept at using a fish knife.

Did not exactly resonate with
audiences.

Live unknown,
make your wants few.

Did you know
you would live long enough
to see the size of your prostate
exceed the size of your ego?

Operators are standing by.

Misery is Optional.

I apologize for the inconvenience.

Bull Market Baroque.

Knowledge
is learning something every day.
Wisdom
is letting go of something every
day.

Do not get in the way of your
enemies
when they are in the process of
self-destruction.

Beauty fades.
Dumb is forever.

The lucky sperm syndrome.

People buy things they don't need
To impress people they don't like
With money they don't have.

Churning in his urn.

Ignore half of what people tell
you.
And disregard the rest.

Oh what a tangled web
we weave,
when first we practice
to deceive.

A legend in his own mind.

May your house
always be too small
to hold those who love you.

To be on a boat
is like being in jail,
with the added possibility
of drowning.

Wisdom
is knowing what to overlook.

I am not here for a long time…
I am here for a good time.

No better friend…
No worse enemy.

Like Grandma's night shirt,
it covers everything.

He can talk a dog off a meat
wagon.

Behind every great fortune,
there is a great crime.

If you don't know how to cook,
You have to know where to buy.

A second marriage
is the triumph of hope
over experience.

Ending is better than mending.

Willingness in principle
to compromise
must never be confused with
willingness to compromise on
principle.

Live by the ocean.
Swim in the pool.

Ego is the anesthesia
which deadens
the pain of stupidity.

Rock bottom
can be a good foundation.

Never let your schooling
get in the way
of your education.

One taco short of a combination
platter.

His elevator does not go to the
top.

A Gentleman never notices.

Separation of Church and State.
Keep the wilderness
out of the garden.

It is better to be over the hill
than under it.

Do not resist growing old.
Many are denied the privilege.

A healthy year and many of
them.

You are not as young
as you used to be.
But you are not as old
as you are going to be.

Old Age
May it always be ten year older
than I am.

Jumbo/Shrimp
Fun/Run
Microsoft/Works

Pride is the burden
of a foolish person.

Answer with delicate refusal.

Middle Age:
Exchanging emotions
for symptoms.

If you are not a Liberal in your
youth,
you have no heart.
If you are not a Conservative as
an adult,
you have no brain.

History will be kind to me
because I intend to write it.

Just because you are Paranoid
does not mean they are not after
you.

It need not be described with such accuracy.

Grief is love
with nowhere to go.

Organ Recital:
Referring to conversations
regarding health issues.

If you want a friend in
Washington,
get a dog.

Not a creative bone in that body.

A raspberry seed in your denture.

What could possibly go wrong?

Whenever people agree with me,
I always feel I must be wrong.

Some need not know anything
about a subject
in order to give an informed
opinion.

Agree to Disagree.

Disagree without being
disagreeable.

Sunshine is the best disinfectant.

Looking for a steal,
not just a deal.

Leap and the net will appear.

If you walk in another's track,
you leave no footprints.

The price of anything
is the amount of life you
exchange for it.

If not you, then who?
If not now, then when?

Plan ahead;
It wasn't raining when Noah built
the ark.

The best thinking
is done in solitude.
The worst
has been done in turmoil.

Don't wait for your ship to come
in.
Row out and meet it.

Some people complain.
Some people just do it.

Reputations are not built
on what you are going to do.

Moderation is a fatal thing.

Nothing succeeds like excess.

There is no more miserable
human being
than one in whom
nothing is habitual
but indecision.

A good plan
violently executed now
is better than a perfect plan
next week.

It is better to be a "Has Been"
than a "Never Was."

A wrong decision is not forever;
it can be revised.
The losses from a delayed
decision
are forever;
they can never be retrieved.

To be nothing is the result of
doing nothing.

There is no such thing as a good
excuse.

Success=Energy well directed.

What matters
is not the size of the dog
in the fight.
It is the size of the fight
in the dog.

A man is not finished when
defeated.
He's finished when he quits.

After all is said and done,
death is still an incomprehensible,
devastating experience
to those who are left behind.
After all the rationalization,
the heart still cries.
It should.

Winners never quit.
Quitters never win.

A secret is whispered everywhere.

Progress
might have been all right once…
It has gone on far too long.

Life is just one damned thing after
another.

A critic
is a person who knows the way
but cannot drive the car.

Three kinds of Lies:
Lies
Damned Lies
Statistics.

There is no such thing
as bad publicity.
Except your own obituary.

Vote for the man who
promises the least.
He will be the least disappointing.

"Dahling"
The start of not remembering
names.

Middle Age:
When the narrow waist
and the broad mind
change places.

Youth
would be an ideal state
if it came a little later in life.

Sleep.
Pleasant and safe to use.

Be nice to people
on your way up.
You will meet them
on your way down.

It is better to be lucky
than to be good.

If you steal from one,
it is plagiarism.
If you steal from many,
it is research.

The optimist proclaims
we live in the best
of all possible worlds.
The pessimist
fears it is true.

Jealousy = Fun you think you
had.

Better to keep your mouth shut
and appear stupid,
than to open it
and remove all doubt.

Too bad all the people
who know how to run the country
are busy driving taxi cabs
and cutting hair.

Oh for just one more conference
regarding the eradication
of all conferences.

Between two evils…
Pick the one not tried before.

A memorandum is written
not to inform the reader
but to protect the writer.

Two tragedies in life:
1) Not to get your heart's desire.
2) To get it.

Inside every seventy year old
is a thirty-five year old asking:
"What Happened?"

When you are young, you are
blamed for crimes you never
committed.
When you die, you get credit for
virtue you never possessed.
It evens itself out.

No matter how old the parent,
they watch their middle-age
children
for signs of improvement.

The whiter the hair,
the more believable you become.

No person
has a good enough memory
to be a successful liar.

Being powerful
is like being a lady.
If you must tell you are,
you are not.

If a fool and his money
are soon parted,
Why are there so many
rich fools?

Experience comes
when one is too old
to take advantage of it.

As soon as people are old enough
to know better,
they don't know anything at all.

Today is the tomorrow
you worried about
yesterday.

There is no answer.
There is not going to be an
answer.
There never has been an answer.
That is the answer.

An optimist sees an opportunity
in every calamity.
A pessimist sees a calamity
in every opportunity.

I don't like money;
however,
it quiets my nerves.

Winning is everything.
The only ones to remember you
when you come in second
are your spouse and your dog.

Failure: Try to please everyone.

Viewing a fine home.
Communist: "No man should
have so much."
Capitalist: "All men should have
as much."

The meek shall inherit the earth,
but not the mineral rights.

Die young,
and as late as possible.

Life is an echo.
What you send out, you get back.

Likewise:

Life is a mirror.
What you see is what you get.

Not young enough
to know everything.

Old:
Believe everything.
Middle Age:
Suspect everything
Young:
Know everything.

Common Sense;
Not so common.

In every age
"The Good Old Days"
are a Myth.

Sarcasm
is the greatest weapon
of the smallest mind.

Experience
is the name given
to the greatest mistakes.

Genius
is knowing how to conceal your
sources.

It is better to be approximately
right
than precisely wrong.

Polish
does not change quartz into a
diamond.

Talking,
repeat what you know.
Listen,
and often learn something.

Ego Trip:
A journey to nowhere.

A good architect can improve
the looks of an old house
merely by discussing
the cost of a new house.

A person asking for advice generally has a mind made up and is looking for confirmation rather than counseling.

Life is like a roll of toilet paper. The closer it gets to the end, the faster it goes.

You cannot shake hands with a closed fist.

When an old person dies, a library is lost.

There is no right way
to do something wrong.

Three can keep a secret,
if two of them are dead.

When I count my blessings,
I count you twice.

Remedy for anger
is delay.

When everyone kicks with the
right foot,
you kick with the left foot.

My own business
always bores me to death.
I prefer other people's.

Anyone can make history.
Only great men
can write history.

I never forget a face.
But in your case,
I would be glad to make an
exception.

I have never killed a man,
but I have read many an obituary
with a great deal of satisfaction.

It does not matter how things
were.
What matters
is how you remember them.

When your horse dies,
it is time to dismount.

Do not hate your enemies.
You will destroy yourself.

The most important investment
you will ever make
is the relationship
with family and friends.

Any Port in a Storm.

A stopped clock
is correct twice a day.

A correct choice
is not necessarily a right choice.

Success
is moving from failure to failure
with no loss of enthusiasm.

Just float.
Not every pebble is a boulder.

You will never get over it.
But you will get through it.

Lead by walking around.
Not from behind a desk.

The trouble with socialism
is that eventually
you run out of other people's
money.

How do you know
when _____ is lying?
When _____
opens his/her mouth.

Some books consist of writing.
Others are simply typing.

A writer puts words together.
Every now and then
they are in the right order.
To give the world a nudge.

Dying is easy.
Parking is hard.

Get it from the horse's mouth.
Not from some horse's ass.

A legend in his own mind.

If you want to be the best,
you have to beat the best.

One of the very nicest things
about life
is the way we must stop
whatever it is we are doing
and devote our attention to
eating.

Both politicians and diapers
need to be changed often,
and for the same reason.

We all have the strength
to endure the misfortunes
of others.

I have always been interested in
people.
But I have never liked them.

A manuscript, like a fetus,
is never improved by showing it
to somebody before it is
completed.

The only reason
people get lost in thought
is because it is unfamiliar
territory.

What this country needs
is more unemployed politicians.

I drink
to make other people more
interesting.

Democracy
substitutes election
by the incompetent many
for appointment
by the corrupt few.

The most dangerous place in
Washington
is between a politician and a
camera.

Don't scold them.
School them.

Some people should be enjoyed,
with caution.

There are no Atheists in Fox
Holes.

The less time you have to work
in,
the more things get done.

Keep your words soft and tender.
Tomorrow you may have to eat
them.

Opportunities are never lost;
Someone will take
the ones you miss.

To ignore the facts
does not change the facts.

Middle age
is when you have met so many
people
that every new person
reminds you of someone else.

No good deed goes unpunished.

Of all noises,
music is the least disagreeable.

Elderly man
seeking a rich Widow;
Nurse with a Purse.

Music with dinner
is an insult both to the cook
and the violinist.

When it is not necessary
to make a decision,
it is necessary
not to make a decision.

Though he is not naturally
honest,
he is sometimes,
by chance.

What is on your mind?
If you will allow the
overstatement?

The two hardest things to handle
are failure and success.

It is a rare person who wants to
hear
what he does not want
to hear.

The only normal people are
the ones you don't know very
well.

Q: Is sloppiness in speech
caused by ignorance or apathy?
A: I don't know and I don't care.

If I had known
I was going to live this long
I would have taken better care of
myself.

We do not know
a millionth of one percent
about anything.

If today was a fish,
I would throw it back in.

War is a series of catastrophes
that result in a victory.

Better to be a "Nouveau Riche"
than never to have been "Riche"
at all.

Behind every great fortune,
there is a great crime.

I did not know he was dead;
I thought he was British.

Somebody left the cork out of my
lunch.

Academic politics
are so vicious
precisely because
the stakes are so small.

Life does not begin
at conception or at birth.
Life begins
when the kids leave home
and the dog is dead.

Religion is what keeps the poor
from murdering the rich.

After all is said and done,
more is said than done.

I was born at night.
Not last night.

A Gentleman never notices.

Progress
might have been all right once.
But it has gone on far too long.

I would like to have kids one day.
But just for that day.

He lies
not because it is in his interest.
He lies
because it is in his nature.

What is the question?
There is no question.
There is no answer.

I have never killed anybody.
But I have read many obituaries
with delight.

Never miss a good chance to shut
up.

The best way
to keep one's word,
is not to give it.

Good advice
is one of those insults
that ought to be forgiven.

It is no longer
a question of staying healthy.
It is a question
of finding a sickness you like.

I don't deserve this award.
But I have arthritis
and I don't deserve that either.

I get my exercise
acting as a pallbearer
to my friends who exercise.

To eat is human.
To digest, divine.

Manuscript:
Something submitted in haste
and returned at leisure.

Some manuscripts
are both good and original.
The parts that are good
are not original
and the parts that are original
are not good.

There are two kinds of books:
Those that no one reads,
and those that
no one ought to read.

Q: How many people work here?
A: About half.

What do you think of the singer's
execution?
I am all for it.

There is so much to be said in
favor of modern journalism.
By giving us the opinions
of the uneducated
it keeps us in touch with the
ignorance of the community.

I am so miserable without you.
It is almost like having you here.

After twelve years of therapy
my psychiatrist said something
that brought tears to my eyes.
He said: "No hablo Ingles."

Even if you are on the right track,
you will get run over
if you just sit there.

If it were not for the last minute,
nothing would get done.

Friends may come and go.
Enemies accumulate.

Women
who seek to be equal with men
lack ambition.

Good breeding consists of
concealing how much we think of
ourselves
and how little we think
of the other person.

Charm
is a way of getting the answer
"yes"
without asking a clear question.

A relationship
is what happens between two
people
who are waiting
for something better to come
along.

Never invest in anything
that eats or needs repairing.

Nothing matters very much,
and hardly anything
matters at all.

Force of collapsing perception.

Better an end with horror,
than horror
without an ending.

Not young enough to know
everything.

Old age is not for sissies.

Death
is just a distant rumor to the
young.

Idealism
is what precedes experience;
Cynicism
is what follows.

Always forgive.
Never forget.

Never complain.
Never explain.

Most people
are more interesting
when they stop talking.

The opposite of talking
is waiting.

You are what you eat.

Never give a party
if you will be the most
interesting person there.

Never mistake endurance
for hospitality.

A gentleman
is a man who can play the
accordion
but refrains from playing.

He does not say much,
and when he does...
He does not say much.

Truth
is shorter than fiction.

Truth
is more of a stranger than fiction.

Truth
is the safest lie.

Criticism is prejudice
made plausible.

It is better to be quotable
than to be honest.

You cannot depend on your eyes
when your imagination is out of
focus.

Good judgment comes from
experience.
Experience comes from bad
judgment.

Nobody can make you feel
inferior
without your consent.

Glory is fleeting
but obscurity is forever.

What is this,
an audience
or an oil painting?

Only two things are infinite,
the universe and human stupidity.
The former
continues to be uncertain.

I don't know,
I don't care,
and it doesn't make any
difference.

Facts often get in the way of the
truth.

The optimist
proclaims that we live
in the best of all possible worlds.
The pessimist
fears this is true.

Unbidden guests
are often most welcome
when they are gone.

There is no answer,
There is not going be an answer,
There never has been an answer,
That is the answer.

Money cannot buy friends,
but it can get you
a better class of enemy.

The masks are dropped
in the closing years of life.
Similar to the end
of a Masquerade Party.

Encumbered by Heredity.

So many beautiful, smart, adorable
children in the world.
Where do all the ugly, stupid, dull
adults come from?

Eating an anchovy is like eating
an eyebrow.

Plant carrots in January,
and you will never have to eat
carrots.

If you don't take care of your
body,
where will you live?

The art of medicine,
like that of war,
is murderous and conjectural.

Voters want a fraud
they can believe in.

A penny saved
is a Congressional oversight.

Every hero
becomes a bore at last.

Violence never solved anything.

Exercise daily.
Eat wisely.
Die anyway.

You can be sincere
and still be stupid.

The closest anyone
ever comes to perfection
is on a job application form.

No style
is better than any style.

Just because I yell at you,
does not mean
I am angry with you.

Military justice is to justice,
what military music
is to music.

When passions are most
inflamed,
Fairness and Justice
are most in jeopardy.

Truth is stranger than fiction,
and fiction is based on reality.

A face in need of a good punch.

Stuff expands to fill the space.

He has severe back problems,
from too much
Social Climbing.

Death
is nature's way of telling you
to slow down.

Here's your hat,
what's your hurry?

We grow too soon old
and too late smart.

Thanks to the Interstate Highway
System,
it is now possible to travel
from coast to coast
without seeing anything.

Response to "Have a Nice Day."
Thank you,
but I have other plans.

It is not enough to succeed.
One's friends must also fail.

The truth is hypothetical.

True knowledge
exists in knowing
that you know nothing.

Events are stronger
than the plans of men.

Good writers borrow.
Great writers steal.

A man can bear the loss of his
father
with equanimity.
But the loss of his inheritance
will drive him to despair.

Prescription for happiness:
Live unknown,
make your wants few.

Know yourself.
Nothing in excess.

Reality
is merely
an illusion,
albeit
a persistent one.

However pure your voice,
better to let silence reign.

Everyone is striving
for what is not
worth having.

Fortune
brings in some boats
that are not steered.

Made in the USA
Middletown, DE
27 March 2021